"In this collection of heartfelt poems, Tami explores the challenges and joys of living with a disability. She shares her challenges and resilient spirit with raw passion. It's evident that the emotional aspects of disability, such as isolation, stigma, acceptance, and empowerment have shaped her and made her the empath she is today. Through her honest and lyrical words, she invites readers to identify with her struggles and celebrate her triumphs. *Poems for A Memory* is a book for anyone who has faced hardship and overcome it, or who wants to understand the perspective of someone who has."

—Pammela Savage, Director Data & AI Solutions,
Financial Services, Microsoft

"Tami's poetry delves into the depths of the human experience, laying bare emotions that will resonate with every reader's soul. With raw honesty, she courageously pours her heart onto the pages, capturing the essence of vulnerability. Each line echoes with relatable feelings, reminding us all of the power of authenticity and the bravery it takes to embrace our truths. May this book help us all embrace our truths!"

—Gillian Stollwerk Garrett, Founder and CEO of Gilly's Organics and
host of Everyday Rockstars, the Podcast

"What a treasure of talent, pain, inspiration, and beauty! Tami has poured her heart and soul into this collection of poems that will make you pause, think, laugh, and raise your fist in fury—or in alliance. A rousing read!"

—Kyra Robinov, award-winning author of
Red Winter, HiSTORY and *Urge to Rome*

Praise for *Poems for A Memory*

"Tami is a lifelong activist and this foray into poetry demonstrates her multifaceted approach to advocating for her community not just in the halls of Congress, where I met her, but for those willing to read a writer speaking for millions seeking respect, inclusion, and understanding."

—**William Cunningham**, former Congressional candidate and former U.S. Senate healthcare policy staffer and House Oversight Investigator.

"Through Tami Luchow's heartfelt and vivid poetry, *Poems for A Memory* captures the essence of inclusion, inviting readers to see the world through diverse perspectives. Luchow's moving poems honor the dignity of every individual and leave readers better than they were before."

—**Lisa Damour**, PhD, New York Times bestselling author of *Untangled: Guiding Teenage Girls Through the Seven Transitions into Adulthood* and more.

"These poems embody the frustration of the unseen, the unheard, and the discounted. They're filled with urgency and dismay. This is the voice of a person with something to say worried that no one is listening—at once concerned and distressed, but still hopeful that maybe tomorrow we will do better. Once you take them in, you will look closer, you will hear more clearly, and you just may find your own voice. Very inspiring."

—**Adam Lenain,** author of *Last of the Famous International Playboys*

"Tami's poems invite us to consider our own contributions to the world as it is, without blame or shame. With each page there is a building sense of injustice, and an invitation to ask the question, "how may I have contributed to this, and what might I do to right these wrongs?" Above all, this book offers a welcome perspective for all of us—whether or not we are living with a disability— and a much-needed prescription for a more inclusive world."

—**Kristin Reihman, MD,** author of *Life After Lyme: Revive Your Inner Rock Star* and *Achieve a Full Recovery,* and host of the Healing Grove Podcast/Membership

"This collection of poetry is a much-needed prescription for empathy and respect for differences. Tami's poems offer a vision where we are all seen and heard."

—**Makunda Abdul-Mbacke**, MD, MPH, FACOG, OBGYN, and CEO Women's Rise Institute

"In these powerful poems, Tami compels us to contemplate and embrace our common humanity, sometimes despite and sometimes because of our differences."

—**Sari Granat**, President and Chief Operating Officer, Chainalysis

"Tami's poems brought a tear to my eye one moment and a broad grin to my cheeks the next. I loved the layout of the poems in the book! I felt engaged on every page. I also thought that even though they are clearly personal, the poems speak broadly to the human condition. The desire to be seen and to be loved—it's exemplified by my absolute favorite line "The circle I ask you to join will only be complete with you in it." Tami eloquently makes the case that we should respectfully acknowledge and celebrate our differences."

—**Sara Farley Holland,** JD, former Army JAG and author of *Federal Trial Objections* (Eighth Edition)

"This collection harmonizes rallying calls for justice; declarations of resilience; and deeply vulnerable supplications for respite. It's a collection for when you haven't chosen the cause, but the cause has chosen you."

—**Ciaran Buckley**, Writer, Storyteller

"*Poems for A Memory* is a deeply personal collection that offers an honest glimpse into the author's world. Luchow shares her vulnerabilities and authentic thoughts, making this a true labor of love. Frank and emotionally driven, Poems for a Memory invites readers to connect with the author's unique perspective and embark on a raw and unfiltered journey."

—**Soyung Pak,** author of *Welcome Baby* and *A Place to Grow*

"A beautiful collection of poetry—honest, vulnerable, and brave. Tami pours her heart and soul onto every page."

—**Loren Michelman,** TV Producer, CNN, NBC, Dateline NBC

Poems for A Memory

Tami Luchow

Published by A SEAT AT DIS TABLE PUBLISHING
www.aseatatdistable.com

For ordering information or special discounts for bulk purchases, please visit: aseatatdistable.com

Design and composition by Hue Boost LLC and Tami Luchow LLC
Cover design by Hue Boost LLC
Author photo by Andrew French

Printed in the United States of America

First Edition
ISBN: 979-8-9914223-2-1

Poems for A Memory

Tami Luchow

"Alone we can do so
little; together we
can do so much"

—Helen Keller

Dedication

To my children, I wish each of you happiness, health, and the ability to brush yourself off and start again with grace, grit, and above all to share your beautiful hearts with the world through your smiles and care. Thank you for embodying my biggest blessing in life: to be your mother. May you travel through life knowing that your hearts and souls are my joy. It is my honor and privilege to watch you learn, grow, and follow your dreams.

And to Steve, for believing.

Little Boys

Little boys little boys where have you
run? I take you for granted and in a
blink you are gone.

My love is a constant like a running
stream. I wake with these words from
a fleeting dream.

Always here. Always there.

In my heart is the art of life.

Then, now, forever.

Never gone, really just a new dawn.

For us, always.

Contents

Author's Note

Let me begin by saying THANK YOU for holding a copy of this book
in your hands, or opening a copy of this book on your e-reader, or listening to a
copy of this book in audio form.

I would like you to know the story of how this collection came to be. I have
been holding onto this for a long time knowing it needs to exist beyond me and
being fearful of letting the poems out publicly. Art is like that. It just must be,
and you don't even know how or why.

One morning I woke up before dawn and the words came pouring out of me,
poem after poem. As soon as one was finished the next one began, and a few
hours went by. I was using my phone as the place to capture the poems. They
didn't even feel like they were being written, more like they were being born
and needing to be heard. I then got scared and didn't look at them for months.

I am someone who has been known to have bouts of "perfection paralysis"
followed by "fear of failure"—two states that don't lend themselves to
publishing poetry. And now here we are, I am exposed and these things that
called out to be in the world are here. Please know they are shared with the
hope that on some level someone somewhere feels they are not alone and that
their own life has worth and meaning.

Living as a person with a sometimes visible and sometimes invisible disability
since birth more often than not puts me in my own category, the only one in a
sea of people. It's A LOT. And it has been my life's work to try my best to take
a stand and raise awareness for people with visible and invisible disabilities,
differences, illnesses, and special needs along with their families, friends,
caregivers, and loved ones. For me, these issues have been vital long before the
terms "Diversity, Equity, Inclusion, Accessibility, and Belonging" were part of
the fabric of life. The concept of respecting and valuing people who are
different has been part of my life from the moment that I was born. Some of
these poems touch on these issues. Others are still struggling to get out of my
mind and onto the page. Most of all, they come from my heart and any errors
are my own.

Respect

Do you hear my heart

Do you see my soul

Do you feel my pain

Do you value my input

The world moves in ways that aren't

accessible that aren't acceptable

that aren't accepting yet here I am here we are

We exist

Existing brings pain yet we have value

Our souls should fly

Our hearts still beat

Our input should be respected

I am a seeker

This is what seekers seek

An Existence with RESPECT

SEEPING

WORDS COME OUT LIKE BLOOD

LIKE SWEAT

SMELLY DIRTY

NUISANCES

NO ONE WANTS THE CLEAN UP

PORES

MOPS

BANDAGES

AWASH WITH FEELINGS THAT DON'T FIT

DON'T JIVE WITH THE POSITIVE OUTLOOK

WILL THE MESS MAKE A DIFFERENCE

WILL THE MESS FINALLY GET SEEN AND HEARD

MAYBE BEING NICE AND SMILEY IS OVERRATED

SEEPING THROUGH IS FRUSTRATION

BUT UNDERNEATH HOPE STILL EXISTS I PROMISE

Emotions

If I speak up I'm too **angry**

If I say something needs changing I'm a
problem

If I act up to make change I'm **ruffling**
feathers

If I take a stand I'm **rocking** the boat

If I'm repeating myself I'm the crazy
person for continuing to **try**

If I'm **screaming** to be heard I'm out of
control

If I'm pensive I'm seething **inside** and
it's eating me up

If I'm **laughing** don't think it's because
something's so funny, it's often a ruse

If I'm writing it's mainly when I'm sad
and my words aren't **valued**

If I'm **silent** watch out things have been
brewing and stewing and emotions will run
high

Hope

Laughing through pain and believing that there will be light on the other side.

Crying big fat ugly tears and letting them flow believing that the release is cathartic in and of itself.

Pushing through pain because there's no other choice and believing that the pain will someday subside.

Rolling with the flow even as the flow feels like it will drown you with its waves and its weight and believing that your own strength deep inside will be the raft you need to make it.

Breathing deeply even when you feel like you can't catch your breath and believing that the stress and the turmoil and the trauma of it all will abate and you will learn from it.

Praying that there is something larger than yourself and all of us that will somehow guide one through the pain and the suffering to a place where believing in goodness and integrity and compassion really do exist.

Hoping that the lessons you've learned and the lessons you try to teach will be uncovered and discovered all the while believing that holding onto hope really is the only way to live through it all.

That is hope.

Faith

I want to believe in a higher power.

But why? I ask.

I want to have faith that I will learn and grow from the hard times.

But why do things have to be so hard? I ask.

I want to trust in my own strength at my heart's center when I feel most alone.

But why do we have to endure such despair? I ask.

I want to understand why it seems that some lives are hit with tough times again and again.

But why are others spared? I ask.

I want to show that I am strong and I have empathy and care and understanding of the plight of others.

But why must I hurt so hard when I have empathy? I ask.

I want to live in the space where I trust my own instincts.

But why have so many ignored me and maligned me and shunned me, or even worse simply discounted me in my otherness? I ask.

I want to have faith.

Overflowing

After 50 years. Get over it. Move on. That ship has sailed. But it hasn't. There was a pause. There was a pandemic. It's happening now. There's still value. There's still time if we make time. There's still a chance if we want it. Now I'm overwhelmed. I'm bursting because I've held so much in for so long. Or rather I've done for others for so long Then I fell down harder than ever before. Getting up wasn't just dusting myself off and starting all over again. It was more pain. It was anxiety. It was heart racing.   It was being misdiagnosed. And ignored. And gaslighting. And worse. But I dug deep and after so many months maybe years of digesting, disseminating and taking in the micro aggressions, the misogyny, the ableism, the devaluation. I found my own truest way always there pushed down and ready to rise. "My Byself" overflowing here and now. A self not always welcome. Often there's no room for her, no bed, no space in the house. She finds her people. She finds her place to gather herself. So she may overflow where valued. So she may overflow where needed. Even when the value and the need isn't yet known by others. Even when others don't want to look in the mirror. The mirror overflows with light, with truth, with certainty of the larger goals.

TEARS

Too
many
are
wasted
because they
are hidden or if
seen they are deemed
weak

Too many are shed in the name of
righteousness but in the face of ignorance
and misguided help

Too many are held in because if allowed to flow one would
overwhelm and drown in the vast sea —the torrent explodes

Too many are stopped in death that comes too soon, life that
isn't fully led because of lack of access lack of care lack of
health, healing or proper medical conditions

Too many to wipe away or show for fear of weakness being
mistaken for strength, because to cry is to show the
empathy for the human spirit to care for the cause to care
for the other when the other's name and place is
unknown but still knowable still painful still worthy of
the fight

The tear signifies togetherness of spirit of
strength of value of being

Not for profit not for show
for humanity

Safety

Being heard   Being seen

Being valued

Being cared for   Being respected

Being cherished

Being touched   Being loved

Being in the room

Being hugged   Being invited

Being accepted

Being included   Being wanted

Safety is all these and so much more.
We have much work ahead for a
world that is safe.

Disability

Disparaging   Soft

Blistered   **Dis**

Unkempt   Cracked

Poor

Hardened   Broken   **Disillusioned**

Disgruntled

Painful   Neglected

Beaten   Forgotten

Ignored   Mistreated

Mismanaged

Scattered

Unhealthy   Silenced

Trampled

Misbegotten

Sequestered

Devalued

Maligned

Hopeless   Alive

Heartsick   Brave   Messy

Puss-filled

Unfit

Hard

Unsuccessful   Lazy

Discouraging

Bloody

Still here, always have been, always will be.

People with Disabilities thrown out of the biblical cities because of impurities, hidden away so as not to mess up bloodlines and marriage chances, yet we exist, disabilities and all.

Can you just?

Can you just look at me and really see me?

Can you just look inside yourself and see the pain you're causing?

Can you just understand that I'm trying so hard to breathe today and I can't do anything more?

Can you just hold my hand and share the pain I feel for the whole world's suffering?

Can you just begin to see what it's like to have all these thoughts in my head spinning around?

Can you just have faith that sometimes the roller coaster of life causes each of us to do things at different times and in different ways?

Can you just trust that we're on the ride together and that's what counts?

Can you just know that when I mess up it's usually because I'm trying to aim high?

Can you just sit beside me and know I wish I could help you in all the ways possible, but I don't even have the right words so a hug is all I can offer?

Can you just see that price tags and net worths aren't what matters as our loved ones fight for every breath?

Can you just know that sometimes standing up for oneself is the bravest act of all?

Can you just feel the muzzle that's on me when I hear injustice right nearby and hold back so I don't rock the boat and cause problems?

Can you just walk next to me and share some time because that's more valuable than any fancy gift or anything?

Can you just open your soul enough to hear me say I'm sorry and perhaps say you're sorry too?

Can you just feel the weight of life deeply enough to understand what empathy for another feels like?

Can you just please?

FAMILY

VALUED FOR WHO WE ARE
UNSEEN FOR WHO WE ARE

MONETIZED AND PRIORITIZED
PENNILESS AND CAST ASIDE
HELPING AND VALUED
HURTING AND IGNORED

MOMENTS OF CONNECTION
MOMENTS ADRIFT
ALONE AMONGST SO MANY
UNITED WITH SO FEW
MAYBE ...

FAMILY IS A UNIVERSE OF FAR AWAY GALAXIES RACING TOWARD EACH OTHER IN INFINITE COMBINATIONS BECAUSE OF THE BLACK HOLE THAT IS OUR UNKNOWABLE SOULS; OR ARE THEY JUST BEYOND REACH AND YEARNING FOR THAT CONNECTION TO SEE A SHOOTING STAR OR A COMET IN THE NIGHT SKY JUST ONCE TOGETHER THAT WOULD BE ENOUGH TO CREATE A NEW PLACE OF WHOLENESS IN A MOMENT OF TIME!

The Paradoxes

To be seen **but not heard**

To be visible **but invisible**

To be heard **but not understood**

To be present **but not counted**

To be in the room **but alone**

To be human **but not valued**

These are the tragic paradoxes.

Words

Tumbling since before time
Thoughts to be shared
Moments to be captured
Things to be said
Things to be heard
But people listen without hearing
Or they say things they don't mean
What has value without a price
The meaning was always there
The importance never changed
Just perspective
Just a different platform
Just because there's a chance for awards
Meaningless in the face of the larger need
Words need actions
Actions need a place to exist
Words mean one life matters

JUSTICE

If I can get in so should they
If we all can't get in no one is free
If the room isn't open then it is a prison
Of minds of beliefs of misguided values
Justice for all or Justice for none
Big words small deeds
Small words big deeds

Things don't matter if any one human
is oppressed or undervalued or
misrepresented
The fight is necessary
The fight is exhausting
It's everywhere
It's timeless
It's now
Justice must prevail

ATROCITIES SHARED
CARELESSLY
MOST OFTEN WITH CARE

Toughen Up
Keep your head held high
Stay strong
Chin up
Brush yourself off
Pick yourself up
Grace
Grit
Resilience
Live and Learn
Things Happen For Reasons
Suck It Up, Buttercup
Thick Skin
Grow Up
Turn the other cheek
You're better than this
Don't give in
Never show pain
Don't cry
Emotions are weakness
Tears are a waste

Truth

They say the truth hurts

Speaking truth hurts more

Truth can be **brutal**

Truth can be painful

One person's truth causes another person's wrath

Truth to **power**

Truth is bravery

Truth causes friction

Truth makes enemies

Truth hurts

Truth helps

Truth can be a harsh mirror

Truth has power to help

Being **truthful** is enlightening

Sharing truth is brave

Speaking truth is scary

Truth can **heal** IF heard and valued

The IF is the key

Speaking truth with every step

Steps hurt, truth hurts, silence equals death.

Lenses

Life is all about lenses.

The way we interact in the world around us is through lenses.

Some of us are empaths and the weight of wearing so many
lenses exhausts and emboldens us.

Some of us are so stuck in our own lens that not only can't we
see the situations of others we actively fight against their views.

All the degrees in the world can't make someone actually
understand another's lens.

Some have glasses with rose colored lenses.

Other lenses have been cracked and broken
and stomped on by life.

Still others don't even have the means for any lenses
broken or new.

Lenses are literal.

Lenses are figurative.

See me through my lens.

I'm doing the best I can to see you through your lens.

All we can do is try to see.

Lenses.

Honey do you...

Honey do you know I'm trying so hard?

Honey do you know I love you so much it hurts?

Honey do you know I wish I could take away all your pain?

Honey do you know I walk with you even as you're far away?

Honey do you know I wish I could take back some things
I've said?

But as we all know you can't put toothpaste back in the
tube, you can just do your best to clean the mess.

Honey do you know you are valued?
You are, by me.

Honey do you know you are cherished?
You are, by me.

Honey do you know all I do is for you?

Honey do you know how hard it is to write words and finally
have others read them?

Honey do you know that it's true you get more from me
when I get more from you?

Honey do you know I will keep on trying?

Honey do you hear me?

Waking up and smiling anew.
Getting dressed even when it feels like Mt. Everest.
Feeding the kids when no one shows up for you.
Getting the bills paid when it feels
like a shell game.
Opening the mail when it's full of medical bills that are
monetary particles of more cause for pain.

Knowing that you don't believe anyone who says
money doesn't make life easier— anyone who says
that has never had to decide NOT to get something
medically necessary because they don't
have the funds.

Lifting a barbell is nothing compared to lifting one's
spirit in the face of insurmountable challenges.
Doing 30 reps pales in the face of 30 steps when the
ground beneath your feet has shifted because your
feet are no longer there or no longer working; or your
neurons are firing and the words aren't coming out
sensibly and your brain is intact just locked in.
That is a fraction of what forging ahead
with fortitude means.

That is Strength.

FRIENDSHIP

Making time for another.
Calling someone on their garbage.
Believing even when life is hardest.
Just listening.

Hearing pain without judgment.
Opening your home.
Giving of one's heart.
Speaking truth when truth needs to be heard.
Doing the hard stuff.
Being there when family is not.
Encompassing the messy stuff when most
vanish.

Letting the emotions flow, without recourse,
but with care and honesty.
Showing one is valued.
Taking a walk.
Answering a phone call.
Cheering not at the win, but for surviving the
loss.

Offering a safe space.
Caring for the other.
Sharing the blessings of a meal together.
Laughing in the face of pain.
Making memories.

Sometimes being out of touch for a long time,
but picking up immediately and being there.

Friendship is earned, chosen, and cherished
most deeply.

PAIN

Ugly and scary and hard and shameful
Pain is not wanted not welcomed not chosen
Difficult, sweaty, bloody, raw like rubbing of skin
against a stone
Sores happen and ooze and break down and cause
new pain

Deeper in the physical and still further embedded in
the soul

Sometimes on the outer edge and the tip of the
tongue and other times pushed and prodded and
stuffed inside because the escape is too painful
itself a new wound and a new way to allow still
More
Hurt
In
The body
And the mind must at once handle the pain and stay
strong and also allow it to flow through and not take
hold because it will eat you up inside and cause still
other harm

Most don't even
Fathom
They just don't comprehend
And really no one could unless a fellow warrior
Though each often feels so alone and often is made
to feel that somehow they're not tough enough when
really those speaking have no idea
Judgment adds more pain beyond the physical

Multimedia

I want these to be seen as brush
strokes on canvas;

As pencil marks on paper;

As key strokes on a keyboard;

As musical notes to be sung, ♪ ♫
listened to;

As images to be seen, experienced;

As videos to be viral;

As dances to be choreographed;

As words to be heard, read, felt;

To be valued, to count, to amount, to
matter;

Multiple mediums; multimedia.

Exist

Who are you?
Who am I?
What are we?
Do you see me?
Can you actually hear me?
Words are spoken, is meaning exchanged?
What do I see?
I can see tears flow
I can taste their salty make up
Can you really understand why?
How?
Who?
I can feel a pulse quicken —
I can see cheeks get red and veins pop —
Can you truly know what's spoken?
What?
When?
This is a solitary existence.
This needs a place to be shared —
To be validated —
To be understood —
I exist, we exist.
We are beautiful in our ugliness.
Ugliness that only comes from outside —
No one is born with ideas of beauty and
ugliness just born to breathe cry laugh smile;
born to be and exist.

TOO MUCH

Too helpful
Too caring
Too committed
Too questioning
Too deep
Too intense
Too sensitive
Too empathetic
Too honest
Too painful
Too difficult
Too positive
Too sad
Too anxious
Too upbeat
Too heavy
Too small
Too talkative
Too quiet
Too hokey
Too smiley
Too passionate
Too much
I am all of these and more
Take me or leave me

WATER

THE SOUND OF WAVES SO PEACEFUL AND CALMING

BUT WATER CAN ALSO OVERTAKE AND CAUSE
DROWNING

FINDING THE BALANCE BETWEEN BEING OVERWHELMED
BY THE SWELLS AND BEING ABLE TO FASTEN A RAFT TO
FLOAT AND RIDE OUT THE STORM

SOMETIMES ONLY IN THE SURGE DOES THE IMPOSSIBLY
IMPORTANT THING EMERGE

FINDING ONESELF ALONE IN THE VASTNESS OF BLUE
CONNECTED TO SHORES AROUND THE WORLD

BOBBING IN THE SAME HYDROGEN AND OXYGEN TWO
PARTS AND ONE AND ALTOGETHER NECESSARY

A MIND ADRIFT IN NOTHINGNESS AND AT ONCE
HOLDING ON TO WHAT IS MOST PRECIOUS — ONE'S SELF

WILL THERE BE WATER DAMAGE

OF COURSE THERE ALWAYS IS

THEN WHEN DRIED OUT A NEW PERSON EMERGES

A SURVIVOR YET AGAIN

WITH MORE STORIES TO TELL FOR HAVING TREADED IN
THE DEEPEST, DARKEST

SOMEONE REALLY
SAID THIS TO ME:

"Haven't you done the disability thing enough?"

Just leaving that there.
Let it sink in.
I have lots to say...
I am at a loss for words...
Lots of work ahead.

Will you join the circle?

Acknowledgments

This collection would not be possible without so many people through the years, and any omissions are mea culpa. My Nana, Hazel Berlin Luchow, one of my earliest readers and supporters. Without her, I just would not be who I am today. My Baba, Miriam Treiman Kaptzan Frank Mrantz, also an integral part of my life, especially when it came to reaching for the stars and taking a stand.

And to my mother Anya Kaptzan Luchow Liberman and my father Jed Luchow for believing in me immediately, when many of the experts did not, and to my grandparents not mentioned and on all sides and in all permutations, and each in their own ways dear, Sylvan Luchow, Marcus Frank, Mark Kaptzan, Bella Kaptzan, Mickey Liberman and Saul Liberman, and to my large and extended "his, hers, ours, and then some" family, my aunts, uncles, and cousins, from birth and beyond, first, second, third, and once, twice, whatever, removed, my step-parents, Donald Liberman, Sharon Kaplan Luchow, Jim Twaite and Linda Palumbo, my siblings and their spouses, my nephews and nieces, my in-laws, my family through family, by marriage, continued even after divorce, by re-marriage, for the relationships we have had in years past, and those we still cultivate, multi-generationally, I would not be the human being that I am today through all these years—were it not for you. I send grace to you all.

And to my dearly trusted early readers Marisela Santiago, Steve Sachs, Kyra Robinov and Angela Herrera. And to Karen Milhoua Lightfoot, Tyke O'Brien, Barbara Dorf, Aimee Altschul Latzman, Paula Newman and Jen Sterling Goldstein, and to my friends near and far, old and new, for a season, for a reason, for life, you have touched me, and changed me, and I thank you.

Extra thanks to all the "teachers" in my life, the people who have made me the survivor, the reader, the learner, the investigator, the researcher, the speaker, the writer, and the challenger of the status quo that I am. I have struggled here between the naming of each and every person who has touched me and the fear that I will miss someone and so in the context of care and faith, please know that I know your names and you are here in these pages with me, that means you, book clubs, committee members, volunteers, doctors, nurses, helpers, upstanders among others. I also struggled with the fact that I took so long to birth this that some OGs are no longer in this world to read these words and I hope they know somehow. I am working on my memoir, yes, you heard it here, and I am almost ready to share three other books, that are not poems, so there will be other opportunities to share my care. It is the realization of the ripple effect about which I often speak, may we all be the pebble dropped in the water for good and be a ripple of kindness, for we have the power for good and we often do not know where the ripple goes… So, to the many whose connection has had an impact and a ripple in my life, I give you my gratitude for what you did knowingly, or even unknowingly.

And to those who shared their time and their names by gifting me with their words on the front, back, and inside of this book, your care and your praise mean the absolute world to me, I am in your debt: Makunda Abdul-Mbacke, Ciaran Buckley, William Cunningham, Lisa Damour, Gillian Stollwerk Garrett, Sari Granat, Sara Farley Holland, Adam Lenain, Loren Michelman, Soyung Pak, Kristin Reihman, Kyra Robinov, and Pammela Savage.

And finally, to Helen Keller, my role model from earliest childhood when there was no one alive that I could see, feel, touch, and know who looked like me, your life's example of leadership with grace, grit, courage, humor, and humanity is still my beacon of light each and every day; with special thanks to Mr. James Collins for seeing both of us.

About the Author

Tami Luchow is a speaker, writer, leader, change maker, artist, and a DEIA&B (Diversity, Equity, Inclusion, Accessibility and Belonging) consultant. She runs workshops on leadership, DEIA&B, and advises C-suites, executive leadership teams, and human resource professionals on how to incorporate best practices for belonging and a sense of place into one's corporate culture to increase loyalty and value. Tami is also a motivational speaker at business, universities, schools, camps and religious organizations encouraging others to build more confident, meaningful and successful lives.

She was a journalist for many years with NBC News, first at "Nightly News with Tom Brokaw" and then with "Dateline NBC." Tami was born with a physical disability and later in life was diagnosed with an invisible disability. She uses her life experiences to shed light on the fact that many people move between multiple, under-represented communities.

Tami was a ski racer on an international circuit and uses that competitive spirit to stand up for a community that is often neither seen nor heard in boardrooms. She prides herself on getting her foot in the door and having a seat at the table. Tami is the founder of CARE FOR LIFE AND LIMB, currently on hiatus.

Tami is working on her memoir. Her next two books, *Nice Legs* and *DIS IS SEXY* will be published soon. She is also launching her podcast #ASEATATDISTABLE. Her imprint #ASEATATDISTABLE Publishing is accepting submissions. Tami welcomes you to join her on #THEDISTOUR coming to a city near you soon!

www.tamiluchow.com

Author photo by Andrew French

IDEAS FOR JOINING TAMI'S CIRCLE:
(Your Words Here)

PEOPLE IN MY CIRCLE:
(Your Words Here)

I BELIEVE IN MYSELF:
(Your Words Here)